Good Things Come to Those Who Bring Carrots.

A Coloring Book for Horse Lovers

Dana Bauer

Dana's Doodles
St. Clair, MI
www.danadoodles.com

For Buggy & Lu.

The love of
horses
has early indications.

The most
expensive penny
in the world.

Whoever spoke of love at first sight was talking about a pony.

A school horse
makes more
dreams come true
than
a fairy godmother!

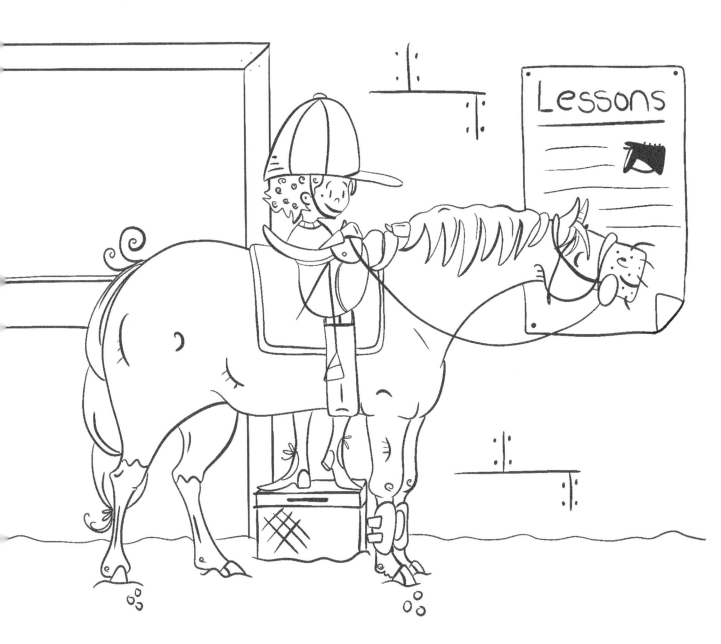

Teaching a child
to ride gives them
the reins to a richer life.

Not all horses respond
to whispering.

Horses put
the royalty
in the
sport of kings.

If you got it,
trot it!

Stall your worries.
Ride your horse.

Some prefer ponies over teddy bears.

The shortest
distance
to the heart
is one horse length.

Brooms are
for amateurs!

Love on the Range

Three day eventers
ride
outside
of the box!

Good things come
to those who
bring carrots!

An apple a day will keep the doctor away, if you take it to the barn and give it to your horse.

A nicker is worth a thousand words.

Have a "little" fun
with a mini!

It is better to ride and fall than never to ride at all!

Horses are the
original
aromatherapy.

When in doubt,
talk to the horse.

Her parents were still waiting for her to outgrow the horse phase.

Draw a doodle:

Notes: